**SCHOLASTIC**

**GRADES K–1**

# First Lessons for Beginning Writers

40 Quick Mini-Lessons to Model the Craft of Writing,
Teach Early Skills, and Help Young Learners
Become Confident, Capable Writers

## Lola M. Schaefer

New York • Toronto • London • Auckland • Sydney
Mexico City • New Delhi • Hong Kong • Buenos Aires

**Teaching** *Resources*

Cover design by Jorge J. Namerow
Cover photograph © Blend Images/JGI
Interior design by Sarah Morrow
Editor: Sarah Glasscock
Copy editor: David Klein

Copyright © 2010 by Lola M. Schaefer
All rights reserved. Published by Scholastic Inc.
Printed in the U.S.A.
ISBN-13: 978-0-545-19570-6
ISBN-10: 0-545-19570-5

1  2  3  4  5  6  7  8  9  10    40    17  16  15  14  13  12  11  10

# Contents

# Introduction

Young students have much to write. They have a wealth of small moments and personal stories to share. These student writers are eager to put their thoughts and ideas on paper. They read and hear new vocabulary and immediately experiment with it. They watch and listen to other writers, adding new strategies to their process. As teachers, we want to keep these students' interest and enthusiasm high. The best way to do that is to offer them a mini-lesson every day during writing instruction. These lessons on craft and genre provide tools that help students improve the quality of their writing.

As teachers of young writers, it is our responsibility to help students do the following:

* mine their own writing topics
* focus on a specific idea
* stretch words and write the sounds they hear
* use expanded vocabulary

* add details
* organize their thoughts
* revise for meaning
* edit for conventions
* work with a writing partner

Mini-lessons help you fulfill these responsibilities. They are brief, highly focused instructional lessons, typically 4–8 minutes in length, although some are shorter or slightly longer. A mini-lesson can explain or demonstrate one feature of the writing process, from brainstorming ideas and providing critical feedback to the craft of writing and proofreading, and classroom writing routines.

Since every classroom has its own procedures and routines, I have not included these kinds of mini-lessons in the book. After reading and using the mini-lessons in this book, you will be able to design your own that fit your classroom routines.

Mini-lessons are like instructional seeds. Each day that you offer a mini-lesson, you're planting the understanding or practice for one aspect of writing. Sometimes, the seed will germinate and sprout immediately in a piece of student writing. Other times it might lie dormant for a week or more before you see evidence of its use. Usually, it takes at least three or four different mini-lessons on the same topic before you see widespread use in student work. Even then, there may be some students who need many more interactions with similar mini-lessons before they employ the demonstrated strategy.

In this book, you will find three different kinds of mini-lessons.

1. **Demonstration:** Either the teacher or a student writer will show through example and explanation how he or she executes one aspect of the writing process. The demonstrator typically shares his or her thinking during the demonstration. It is not enough to show a finished example. Student writers need to know how someone made the choices that led to the piece of developed writing.

2. **Literature-based:** This type of mini-lesson is designed around a passage from a published source. It is important for the teacher to always use text that the students know from previous readings. In this way, they will not be distracted by engagement in a new text and will be able to focus on the purpose of the mini-lesson. During a literature-based

lesson, the teacher uses a mentor text and asks students to read, listen, notice, or list certain features of that text.

3. **Interactive:** The emphasis of this lesson is student engagement in one aspect of writing. It can also be considered a brief practice session. Since students are actively thinking, writing, or revising, they quite often remember the focus of this mini-lesson and use it when writing independently.

To effectively deliver a mini-lesson, ask students to sit close to you so everyone can easily see and hear what is being said and done. This intimate setting makes it easier for you to engage all of the children, as well as monitor their attention and performance.

Remember the purpose of a mini-lesson. It is a teaching tool. Don't expect to see its topic in use in every student's writing that same day, or even that same week. As stated earlier, it sometimes takes many mini-lessons on one topic before students understand the concept and use it in their own writing. Instead, think of a mini-lesson as an invitation. Deliver it as such. By keeping the lesson short and focused, we are offering one tool, one strategy that could make the writing process more enjoyable and productive for each student. At the end of a mini-lesson, always segue into independent writing time by saying something like the following: "Try and find an opportunity today or sometime soon to experiment with this. See if it works for you."

I have found that if you want to get your biggest bang for your mini-lesson, it helps to have a short accountability time at the end of independent writing time. Do not confuse this with "grading" student writing. It is an opportunity to celebrate any attempts students have made to incorporate the provided strategy. For instance, if you offered a mini-lesson on specific word choice earlier, then at the end of writing time say, "During our mini-lesson today, we spoke about the importance of using just the right word to paint a picture. Reread what you've written today and circle one or two words that you think will paint strong pictures in the minds of your readers."

What's interesting about this is that about half of your students will be reading and circling words, and the other half will be reading, erasing, and adding more specific vocabulary. That's fine. Don't let on that you even notice. After a few minutes, ask five or six students to share the words that they circled. By doing this, you are providing a purpose and audience for the mini-lesson of the day. In the future, students will listen and participate even more vigorously during a mini-lesson. And if you don't remember to offer a celebration time after independent writing, they will remind you. Why? Because students have conscientiously used the focus of the mini-lesson and they want to share that with you and the class. As a reminder, I have included this suggestion to follow up with students after independent writing time in a few of the mini-lessons.

Read the table of contents and the different mini-lessons, then select one that will meet your students' needs. Even though I've organized this book to support you in your teaching as the year unfolds, feel free to use the mini-lessons in any order. You are the only one who can make an informed decision about your students. Watch them as they write and choose accordingly.

As you read this book and use the mini-lessons, you will find opportunities to adapt them and create others to meet the needs of your students. The most difficult thing about designing mini-lessons is to keep them short. As teachers, we are often hesitant to trust in such a brief interaction. But do just that. Trust in the power of a focused instructional nugget. Know that your students need many seeds—one day at a time—to build confidence, understanding, and an enjoyment of the writing process.

# Ideas, Ideas

One of the greatest gifts a teacher can give students is the ability to mine their own writing ideas. In kindergarten and grade 1, it is helpful to establish the habit of reflecting and recording. The purpose of this mini-lesson is to create a common space where students can share self-generated writing ideas. This is a precursor to individual writers' notebooks.

> **Type of Mini-Lesson:** Interactive
>
> **Length:**    6–8 minutes
>
> **Materials:**    bulletin board, large piece of paper (6 inches by 3 inches), small pieces of paper (3 inches by 2 inches) for each student, fine-point marker, pencils

## Process

Ask students to join you near the bulletin board.

**Teacher:**    *We are writers, so we want to have the habits of writers. All writers have a place where they keep ideas. Some store them in their computers. Many keep a writer's notebook.*

*Writers who can draw often use a sketchbook to record writing ideas. This year, we're going to have a Writing Ideas bulletin board. It will be a place for all of us to post writing ideas. Let's start right now. I'm going to write the word* family *on this large piece of paper and post it on our board. Let's all shut our eyes and think of someone in our own family.*

Allow 20–30 seconds for children to select a mother, father, sister, brother, grandmother, or grandfather.

**Teacher:**    *I'm going to select my mother. Now, think of one thing that you really enjoy doing with that person. Do you skate together? Do you fish? Do you bake cookies? Or ride bikes?*

Allow a minute for children to think.

**Teacher:**    *I enjoyed reading books with my mother.*

                  *Who would like to share their person and what they like to do together?*

Provide time for four or five students to share. Help them clearly state the person and what they do together.

**Teacher:**    *The person you have chosen is your **who**. My mother is my **who**. What you do together is your **what**. Reading books together is my **what**.*

                  *Here are small pieces of paper for our Writing Ideas board. If you have a **who** and a **what**, take a piece of paper and write those down, or draw a picture showing them. Then we will post your reminders for your ideas on the board under the word* family.

## Classroom Notebook

Some teachers prefer to list ideas in a scrapbook. You can buy an inexpensive scrapbook with large, thick pages. With a bold marker, write a category at the top of each page and invite children to write or draw their idea reminders directly into the book.

Ask students to name the book, using a title that will announce its purpose. Then keep the book and a few fine-point markers out at all times so students not only add entries during brainstorming time but also any time they think of something of value.

## Topics

Other topics to use to generate student ideas include the following:

Pets

Favorite Outdoor Places

Friends

Holidays

Birthdays

# Choice

Students are much more committed to their writing when they are invited to develop their own ideas rather than write to a prompt. The purpose of this mini-lesson is to show students that we value self-expression. We do this by modeling how to select a topic and develop an idea.

**Type of Mini-Lesson:** Interactive

**Length:**     5–8 minutes

**Materials:**     Writing Ideas bulletin board (or scrapbook) from the Ideas, Ideas, mini-lesson (pages 6–7), student journals or writing paper

## Process

Invite students to join you with their pencils and journals (or writing paper) at the Writing Ideas bulletin board you created in the Ideas, Ideas mini-lesson.

**Teacher:**     *Before I write today, I want to reread some of the ideas that we have collected on our board. I know I can write about whatever I want, so I'm going to think about different possibilities.*

*Here someone put up a reminder that we can write about our pet cat and what funny things it does. I have two cats. I could write about how they chase one another up and down the stairs.*

*Or, here is a reminder that we can write about what we liked about a good book. I just finished reading a great mystery book that has lots of surprises in it.*

*This idea reminds us that we can write about something fun we did with a friend. I could write about the time I explored tidal pools with a friend.*

*While I decide what I want to write about today, you can study our reminders and select an idea, too.*

Provide 1–2 minutes for children to think quietly.

*First Lessons for Beginning Writers* © 2010 by Lola M. Schaefer, Scholastic Teaching Resources

**Teacher:**     *I know. I saw the reminder about cats, but I want to write about another animal—Komodo dragons. I just learned some really interesting facts about what and how they eat. I'm going to write* Komodo dragons *on my paper and the word* eat.

*Does anyone want to share with us what you're going to write about today?*

Allow four or five students to share their writing ideas for the day. Help them focus on a specific person or thing and what they're going to write about. Then invite all students to jot their writing ideas in their journals or on paper.

As you excuse students, have them show you their writing idea for the day. If one or two students have not written anything, take a few moments to help them brainstorm an idea.

# Think Back

One way to help emergent and early writers generate their own focused ideas for journal writing is by brainstorming using emotions. The purpose of this mini-lesson is to show students a different way to mine the wealth of writing ideas within themselves.

**Type of Mini-Lesson:** Interactive

**Length:** 8–12 minutes at first, 5–8 minutes after practice

**Materials:** Writing Ideas bulletin board, large piece of paper (6 inches by 3 inches), small pieces of paper (3 inches by 2 inches) or large sticky notes for each student, fine-point marker, pencils

## Process

**Teacher:** *I'd like all of us to shut our eyes and think of a time in our lives when we have been excited.* (Shut your eyes as you continue.) *It might have been a time when your family got a new pet, or when your parents brought home a baby brother or sister, or the first time you fished or rode your bike without training wheels. Let's all be quiet for at least two minutes and think back to an exciting moment. It might have been last week, last month, or last year.*

Wait 2 minutes, then open your eyes.

**Teacher:** *I'm going to share an exciting moment.* (At this time, share an exciting event from your childhood in one or two sentences.) *I remember the day that I caught my first fish. My father and I were at Bixler Lake, and I was seven years old. Who else would like to share an exciting moment?*

Provide time for three to five students to share. Help them keep their summaries short and to the point.

**Teacher:** *We can add these exciting moments to our Writing Ideas board. I'm writing the words* Exciting Moments *on a large piece of paper. Now*

*I'm going to post that on our bulletin board. Here are some smaller slips of paper. If you have an exciting moment, please write the **who** and **what** of that moment on the slip. For instance, my **who** is my dad and me. My **what** is catching my first fish. We will post your idea strips on our board.*

Provide time for a group of students to write their exciting moment ideas and help them post the ideas on the board. If your students want to draw a simple picture as a reminder instead of writing the who and what, that's great, too.

**Teacher:**  *Now I would like all of us to shut our eyes again and think back to a moment when we were frightened. Perhaps you were in a terrible storm or you couldn't find your pet or you were lost.*

Repeat the same sharing and recording process from above.

**Teacher:**  *Look at our board. We collected quite a few writing ideas today. The next time we write in our journals, you might read a few of these to remind you of something important that you'd like to write about.*

## Emotional Moments to Remember

Here are some other emotions that help students remember important moments:

Anger

Joy

Worry

Sadness/grief

Pride

Confusion

Embarrassment

Loneliness

# Breathless Moment

Even though students have witnessed many vivid moments that they could use as writing ideas, they don't always remember them. The purpose of this mini-lesson is to help emergent writers identify past experiences that would be good fodder for descriptive writing.

**Type of Mini-Lesson:** Interactive

**Length:**    8–11 minutes at first, 5–7 minutes after practice

**Materials:**    Writing Ideas bulletin board, large piece of paper (6 inches by 3 inches), a small piece of paper (3 inches by 2 inches) or large sticky note for each student, fine-point marker, pencils

## Process

**Teacher:**    *I'd like all of us to shut our eyes and think of a time when we saw something so beautiful or wonderful that it almost took our breath away.* (Shut your eyes as you continue to speak.) *This might have been a time when you said "Oh" or "Ahhh." You might have seen a bright rainbow or a butterfly emerging from a cocoon. You might have watched a sunset over a lake or a chick hatching from an egg. Maybe you witnessed a mother cat nursing her kittens or the wind scattering flower petals. I'm going to sit quietly and remember one of the most amazing sights I've ever seen.*

Wait about 1–2 minutes, then open your eyes and speak.

**Teacher:**    *I'm going to share with you an image that I remember from long ago.* (At this time, share one of your own breathtaking images in one or two sentences.) *One summer day a hummingbird flew close to my face and hovered in front of my eyes. Who else would like to share a wonderful sight from the past?*

Provide time for four or five students to share. Help them keep their summaries short and focused.

*First Lessons for Beginning Writers* © 2010 by Lola M. Schaefer, Scholastic Teaching Resources

**Teacher:** *How many of you remembered a spectacular image that you've seen? Let's add these images to our bulletin board of writing ideas. I'm writing the words* Beautiful *or* Wonderful Moments *on a large piece of paper. Now I'm posting that on our Writing Ideas board. Here are some smaller slips of paper. If you have an image that you would like to post, please write what you saw in one to four words. For instance, if you saw a mother duck and her ducklings, write* mother duck *and* ducklings. *If you saw the full moon and it glowed yellow, write* full moon, yellow. *I'm going to write the words* hummingbird, close to face. *(Other examples you write might be* my newborn daughter *or* sunflower blooming.*)*

Provide time for a small group of students to write or draw a reminder of their breathless moment and help them post the ideas on the classroom idea board. In days ahead, other students will think of a moment and they can add their ideas at that time.

**Teacher:** *Look at our board. We brainstormed many writing ideas today. The next time we write in our journals, you might read a few of these ideas to remind you of something you've seen that you'd like to write about.*

# List Ideas

Students need to know that they can write about what they know. A good way to help them discover these ideas is by making lists. The purpose of this mini-lesson is to provide a concrete strategy for brainstorming possible writing ideas.

**Type of Mini-Lesson:** Interactive

**Length:** 6–10 minutes

**Materials:** chart paper and marker, overhead and marker, or interactive whiteboard and pen

## Process

**Teacher:** *Sometimes we write about things we do. Other times we write about our families or pets. Today I want to make lists about things we know so we have another way to find writing ideas. I'm going to need your help, of course. For instance, let's begin by listing famous people that you've heard about. I'm going to write the heading "Famous People."*

Start the process by naming two or three famous people that students might know.

**Teacher:** *I'll start. I'm going to write the names "George Washington" and "Christopher Columbus" and "Amelia Earhart." Can you think of other famous people?*

Add four or five names that students call out. They will probably respond with the name of the American president, a famous football or basketball player, Abraham Lincoln, Martin Luther King, Jr., Rosa Parks, and a few others.

Then call on a student to come up and circle the name he or she knows the best. Ask that child: *Why is this person famous? Do you know any other information about this person, such as where he or she lived? What else he or she did?* Provide time for another student to come up and circle a name on the list. Ask that student what he or she knows about the famous person.

*First Lessons for Beginning Writers © 2010 by Lola M. Schaefer, Scholastic Teaching Resources*

**Teacher:** *Let's make one more list today. Let's list animals that we have seen in person. You might have one of these animals as a pet. You might have seen one in a zoo. You might have seen one of these animals at your cousin's or friend's house. I'm going to write the heading "Animals We've Seen in Person" here.*

       *I'll start. I'm going to write* sea star *and* red fox. *Can you tell me some animals you have seen in person?*

As students name animals, add their suggestions to the list. Follow the same procedure from above and provide time for at least two students to come forward and circle something on the list and then tell two facts about that animal.

**Teacher:** *Making lists is one way to brainstorm writing ideas. Once you have a topic, you need to think about your focus—what you want to say about that topic. You might make your own idea list today and choose something that you know about. Then write about that.*

---

### Lots of Lists

Here are a few other ideas for lists that will generate enthusiasm with your emergent writers:

Foods That I Help Make

Things I Collect

Animals That Fly

Objects in the Sky

My Community Helpers

School Workers

What Lives in the Woods

What Lives in the Sea

---

# Write What You Know

Once students have a topic, either from a list or from something they have studied in the classroom, they are ready for a focused writing idea. The purpose of this mini-lesson is to show students how to think of something specific they want to write about their topic. It helps them *narrow* their topic to an idea.

**Type of Mini-Lesson:** Demonstration

**Length:** 7–12 minutes

**Materials:** student-generated nonfiction topic, paper and pencils, chart paper and marker or interactive whiteboard and pen

## Process

Ask students to write their nonfiction writing topics. They may have these listed on the Writing Ideas board, or they may think of a new idea for this lesson. (Possible topics include sharks, firefighters, camping, soccer, or fishing. You want each student to have his/her own topic.)

**Teacher:** *Today we're going to think before we write about our nonfiction topics. I've chosen black bears for my topic. I can't write everything I know about bears. It would take forever, and my audience might get bored. So I want to think about some facts that I know about bears. Let me see.*

*I know what black bears like to eat. I could write about that. I know the kind of habitat they like. I could write about that. I know some of the dangers to black bears. I could write about that. And I know the size of black bears. That's another idea for my writing today.*

*Let me think. I know the most about the different dangers to bears. That will be my writing idea. Let me list a few of those.*

Make a list that all students can see. Think aloud as you write.

**Teacher:** *One danger is hunting. Sometimes people hunt the bears and kill them. I'll write* hunting.

*First Lessons for Beginning Writers* © 2010 by Lola M. Schaefer, Scholastic Teaching Resources

**Teacher:**      *Another danger is that the chemicals people use could poison the bears and their food. I'll write* chemicals.

*One more danger to black bears is the loss of their protected habitat. I'll write* loss of habitat—the places bears like to live.

*I probably won't write about all three of these, but I know that I will write about at least one and maybe two of these dangers.*

*Today, before you write, think about one important fact that you know about your topic. If you can, think of another important fact about your topic. Then decide which one you'd like to write about. Have a focus for your writing.*

# Drawing to Organize

Before students write in their journals, they need to organize their thoughts. Their initial efforts are typically based on reflections of their own experiences. The purpose of this mini-lesson is to show students how to draw a picture with a who and what—the organization for their writing.

**Type of Mini-Lesson:** Demonstration

**Length:**       6–9 minutes

**Materials:**    chart paper and pencil or crayons or interactive whiteboard and pen

## Process

**Teacher:**     *I'm thinking about what I want to write in my journal today. I could write something about my family or pets or an exciting time. I know. I'll write about my Aunt Freeda.*

*When I was ten years old, I would go to her farmhouse in the country and spend a few days. One of my favorite things that we did together was collecting eggs in the barn. I want to write about Aunt Freeda and me taking eggs from beneath the hens.*

*First, I'm going to draw a picture to organize my thoughts. I want my picture to have a **who** and a **what**. My **who** is Aunt Freeda and me. So I will first draw Aunt Freeda and then I'll draw me.*

Use an example from your own childhood and draw the **who**—the people involved in your experience. You will probably be one of the people involved.

**Teacher:**     *Now I want to show **what** Aunt Freeda and I were doing. We were taking eggs from the hens' nests. I need to show each of our arms stretched out and reaching under a hen. I'll draw that now.*

Continue drawing **what** you are doing in this experience. Remember to think out loud so students know how you make your decisions.

**Teacher:** *I'm going to draw baskets on our other arms because that's where we put the eggs that we collected. And I'm going to draw a couple of eggs at the top of the basket.*

Add any other pertinent details to your drawing. Explain your additions by thinking out loud.

**Teacher:** *I'm also going to draw smiles on our faces because this was something that we enjoyed doing together.*

*Now let's look at my picture. I have my* **who**: *Aunt Freeda and me. I have my* **what**: *gathering eggs from the hens' nests. And I have baskets with eggs on our arms and smiles on our faces. I have drawn the important parts of this experience. Now I'm ready to write.*

*As you organize for journal writing today, take time to show your* **who** *and* **what** *in your pictures so you know what you want to write about.*

Once students regularly include the **who** and the **what** in their organizational pictures, you can offer the mini-lesson Drawing With Detail on page 44.

---

### Practice, Practice

Make sure you provide plenty of time for students to organize their thoughts in picture form before you ask them to write. You can have them draw the **who** and the **what** from a different experience each day for 2–3 weeks. Each time, invite students to share their picture with a friend and point to the **who** and the **what**.

---

# Journal Writing

After students learn how to gather ideas and organize their thoughts by drawing a picture, it's time to show them how to write about that idea. The purpose of this mini-lesson is to show emergent writers how to focus their thoughts and write with clarity.

> **Type of Mini-Lesson:** Demonstration
>
> **Length:** 6–10 minutes
>
> **Materials:** an organization picture that contains a **who** and a **what**, chart paper and marker or interactive board and pen

## Process

Hold up or display one of your favorite journal pictures that contains a **who** and a **what**.

**Teacher:** *Today I want to write in my journal. I'm going to use this picture that I drew on another day to remind me of my **who** and **what**.*

*Here, Aunt Freeda and I are standing near the hens in her barn. We are reaching under the hens to collect eggs.*

*I want to make sure that I have our names in my writing, and I want to tell what we're doing. I could write any of these sentences:*

*Aunt Freeda and I are collecting eggs from the hens. Aunt Freeda and I had fun gathering eggs. Aunt Freeda taught me how to collect eggs from the hens. Aunt Freeda and I gathered warm eggs from the hens.*

*I've decided to write this sentence: Aunt Freeda and I gathered warm eggs from the hens.*

Put a magic line (see the Magic Lines mini-lesson on page 27) down for your first word, stretch the word (see the Stretching Words mini-lesson on page 29), and write it. Continue with this process, rereading your writing after the addition of each word until your entire sentence is complete.

**Teacher:** *Look back through the pictures you have drawn. Find one to use for your writing today. Think about your **who** and your **what**. When you can hear a sentence in your mind, make your first magic line and begin to write.*

### More To Say

If your students have been writing in their journals for a few weeks, extend this lesson. In your modeling, write two sentences for your picture. For instance, I could have written:

*Aunt Freeda and I gathered warm eggs from the hens.*

*We carried them to the house in our baskets.*

Our demonstration mini-lessons need to be lures—ways of showing students how they can add meaning by writing more information and details.

# The Who and What

Once emergent writers demonstrate success with focused pictures and the conventions of print, they can draw (prewrite) and write during the same class period. The purpose of this mini-lesson is to help students identify a **who** and a **what** for both their pictures and their writing.

**Type of Mini-Lesson:** Demonstration

**Length:** 5–8 minutes

**Materials:** chart paper and markers or interactive whiteboard and pen

## Process

**Teacher:** *I want to write in my journal today about getting a new puppy. My **who** is a puppy. I need to draw my puppy in my picture. This will help me organize and focus my writing.*

Draw a puppy on chart paper or an interactive whiteboard.

**Teacher:** *Now I need my **what**. What is my puppy doing? He is wagging his tail back and forth. That's what he did when I played with him at the humane shelter. I need to draw his tail wagging back and forth.*

Draw the puppy's tail to the right and again to the left. Add four horizontal lines between the tails to show movement.

**Teacher:** *Now I'm going to write. I want to hear the words in my head before I write my sentence: "The puppy is wagging his tail back and forth." **Who** am I writing about?*

**Students:** *The puppy.*

**Teacher:** ***What** is the puppy doing?*

**Students:** *He is wagging his tail.*

**Teacher:** *Good. I have my **who** and my **what**.*
*Before you draw or write in your journals today, please decide **who** you are writing about and **what** that person or animal is doing.*

## Adding More

For students who have stronger literacy backgrounds, write two sentences and think aloud, for example:

*Why was the puppy wagging his tail?*
*He was happy to play with me.*

or

*He likes playing with me.*

Say: "I'm going to write two sentences."

*The puppy is wagging his tail back and forth.*
*He likes playing with me.*

Close by saying: "Today, if you want, you can write a second sentence that tells us more about your **who** and **what**."

 First Lessons for Beginning Writers © 2010 by Lola M. Schaefer, Scholastic Teaching Resources

# From Topic to Idea

Quite often, students confuse a topic with a writing idea. If you ask, "What are you going to write about?" you may hear, "My bike." Or the response may be, "My brother." Those are topics. An idea is focused. The purpose of this mini-lesson is to show students how to start with a topic and then select a specific focus so their writing pops on the page.

> **Type of Mini-Lesson:** Demonstration/Interactive
>
> **Length:**      6–8 minutes
>
> **Materials:**   chart paper and marker

## Process

**Teacher:**  *I've been reading a lot about elephants lately, and today I would like to write about them. But the topic of elephants is a BIG one. I could write for a whole week and still have more to say. Could all of you help me think of some writing ideas about elephants? Could you help me list specific kinds of information that I could write? For instance, I could write about what elephants eat. Or I could write about how they give birth to live babies. What else? What could be some other writing ideas?*

**Students:**  *You could write about where elephants live.*

*Or you could write about their trunks.*

*You could write about the different kinds of elephants.*

*Why not write about their tusks?*

*How about writing about their size?*

Write down the student suggestions and then display them.

**Teacher:**  *I've written down all of our idea suggestions. I've decided to write about elephant tusks because I know some good facts about tusks. I'm going to describe tusks and tell the different jobs they do.*

*Thank you. I feel better now because I have a focus for my writing.*
*I can now sit and think about exactly what I want to write.*

    *Before you write today, think about your topic. Then find a*
*specific focus—one important thing you want to write about on*
*that topic.*

## Know What You Want to Say

If students are writing about an experience, have them focus with **who** and **what**. If they decide to write about a nonfiction topic such as volcanoes, flowers, snakes, or monsters, have them decide on a topic and then a focus. The tighter their focus, the stronger their writing will be.

# Character and Problem

Children's lives are made of story. It makes sense that as soon as they learn to write, they want to write the stories of their own lives. The purpose of this mini-lesson is to help student writers know that every story starts with a character and a problem, or a job to do.

**Type of Mini-Lesson:** Literature-based

**Length:**      5–8 minutes

**Materials:**   Two published stories that begin with a character and a problem, or a job to be completed. In this lesson I'm using *Ruby Bakes a Cake* by Susan Hill (HarperCollins, 2004) and *Dog and Bear: Two's Company* by Laura Vaccaro Seeger (Roaring Brook Press, 2008).

## Process

**Teacher:**     *We have been reading lots of stories. Every story has two things that it needs. It needs a character: a boy, a girl, a dog, a caterpillar, or even a truck. And a story needs a problem, or a job that needs to be completed. For instance, a boy could be afraid of spiders, and one crawls on his desk at school. Or a girl might have wandered away from her parents at the circus, and now she is lost. Or a squirrel needs to make a nest and has to find materials to build it. Every good story has both of these: a character and a problem, or a job to do.*

*Strong stories introduce the character and the problem at the very beginning. A good story grabs the reader's attention by showing that the character has to work hard or struggle.*

*I'm going to read the first page of a story two times. I want you to be listening for the character: the person, animal, or thing that the story is about. And I want you to listen for this character's problem or the job that needs to be completed.*

Read the first story lead two times. (This is usually the first page or the first few sentences.)

**Teacher:** *Who or **what** is the character of this story?*

For *Ruby Bakes a Cake*, the students will say that the character is Ruby Raccoon.

**Teacher:** *What is Ruby Raccoon's problem or **what** does she need to do?*

Students will say that she wants to bake a cake, but she doesn't know how.

**Teacher:** *Exactly. Ruby is our character, and her problem is that she wants to bake a cake, but she doesn't know how.*

Read the second story lead two times. Repeat the above process. For the story *Dog and Bear: Two's Company*, the students will tell you that there are two characters: Dog and Bear.

**Teacher:** *Which character seems to have a problem?*

Students will tell you that Dog is running away, so he seems to have the problem.

**Teacher:** *Good thinking. This is a story about Dog running away because he is angry with Bear.*

*As you start writing your stories today, remember to write about your character and the problem or job to be completed.*

# Magic Lines

The emergent reader sometimes has difficulty leaving spaces between words. The purpose of this mini-lesson is to show students how to speak what they want to write and, with the use of magic lines, write the words in a way that is easy for them and others to read.

**Type of Mini-Lesson:** Demonstration

**Length:**    5–8 minutes

**Materials:**    chart paper and markers, overhead and markers, or interactive whiteboard and pen

## Process

**Teacher:**    *Today I want to write about the volcano I saw on the news last night. I need to think for a moment about the most important thing that I learned.* (Sit quietly for a moment or two.) *I've decided to write about how high the ash and smoke rose into the air. I could write: "The ash and smoke rose more than 50,000 feet into the air." Or I could write, "The volcano blew, sending ash and smoke high, high, high into the air."*

    *Which sentence is the most interesting to you?*

Repeat the sentence that students select and then draw a horizontal line (magic line) on your paper, transparency, or board that is the proper length for the first word. For this example, I will use the first sentence.

**Teacher:**    *Thank you. My sentence will be: "The ash and smoke rose more than 50,000 feet into the air." I just drew my first magic line. This is a line on which I will write all of the letters in the word* the. *The reason I call it a magic line is that it will magically keep all of the letters in one word on that line. Since the word* the *is a shorter word, I'll make a short magic line. Now I'll write the word* the *on this magic line.*

    *I'm going to repeat my sentence so I know which word comes next: "The ash and smoke rose more than 50,000 feet into the air." Ash is my next word.*

**Teacher:** *That's a small word, too, so I'm going to make another short magic line, but first I need to leave a space between the lines. Writers always leave spaces between their words.*

Draw your second horizontal (magic) line.

**Teacher:** *I'm going to write the word* ash. *I'll read what I have written so far: "The ash."*

*Now I need to hear my sentence again: "The ash and smoke rose more than 50,000 feet into the air."*

*I need to leave another space before my next magic line.*

Continue the process until you've written the entire sentence. At the end of the mini-lesson, say something similar to this:

**Teacher:** *Today, as you're writing, you may want to use magic lines. It's one way to help you leave spaces between your words.*

### Magic Support

Students who need magic lines to help them with spacing will use them. Students who already separate their words may or may not use them. Offer this strategy to your class and encourage students who struggle with spacing to use it. The more you model the use of magic lines, the more likely it is that your students will value them.

First Lessons for Beginning Writers © 2010 by Lola M. Schaefer, Scholastic Teaching Resources

# Stretching Words

Emergent writers need to stretch their words and hear the sounds before they can make meaning. Some students come to school with phonemic awareness. Others need quite a bit of help. The purpose of this mini-lesson is to show children how to stretch and write the sounds that they hear.

**Type of Mini-Lesson:** Interactive

**Length:**      5–9 minutes

**Materials:**      chart paper and marker or interactive whiteboard and pen

## Process

**Teacher:**      *Words are made of letters, and letters make their own sounds. For instance, what letter makes the buh sound at the beginning of the word* bee?

*Yes, the letter* b.

*This year we will be writing many words. Some we will know how to spell. They might be on our word wall, or you might have read them so often that you'll know how to spell them. Many words will be new to us. We will need to stretch these words and write the sounds that we can hear.*

*Let's practice with the word* monster. *Watch my mouth and listen while I stretch that word. Muh-muh-muh-o-n-s-t-e-r.* (Notice that I say the first sound of the word three times.)

*Try it with me, please. Muh-muh-muh-o-n-s-t-e-r.* (As you stretch the rest of the word, go slowly and accentuate as many of the sounds as you can.) *Let's stretch that word one more time. Muh-muh-muh-o-n-s-t-e-r.*

*I'm going to make a magic line here for our word. What letter makes the muh sound at the beginning of the word?*

When a child tells you the letter *m* makes the sound at the beginning of the word, ask him or her to come forward and write a lowercase *m* at the beginning of the magic line.

**Teacher:**   *Let's stretch that word together again. Muh-muh-muh-o-n-s-t-e-r.*
*What other sounds do you hear? What letter makes that sound?*

As students hear some of the other sounds, have them come forward and write the letter that makes that sound on the magic line. When they cannot hear any other sounds, you can add any missing sounds until the word is spelled correctly.

At the beginning of the year, your students may only hear the initial sound. Some may hear the initial and ending sounds. As the year progresses, your students will hear more and more of the sounds in every word they stretch.

**Teacher:**   *As you write today, I hope you stop and stretch your words. Listen for the sounds that you recognize and write those down.*

## Accountability

Engage students in as much stretching as you can, so when they are working independently they have the skills and confidence to write the sounds they hear. Sometimes students become reliant on the teacher and wait for him or her to tell them what to write. Instead, let's provide practice in stretching so they can do this on their own.

# Stretching Star

It's fairly easy for students to stretch words when they're part of a group. They simply mimic what everyone else is saying. It's important for teachers to know that all students have this skill. The purpose of this mini-lesson is to provide an opportunity for all students to be the "lead" stretcher, thereby showing their understanding of the process.

**Type of Mini-Lesson:** Student Demonstration/Interactive

**Length:** 4–8 minutes

**Materials:** chart paper and marker or interactive board and pen

## Process

Select one student to be the "Stretching Star" of the day. Ask this child to stand next to you facing the class.

**Teacher:** *We are going to practice stretching words again. Today our Stretching Star is Spencer.*

*Let's begin by stretching the word* rabbit. *Please watch my lips and listen as I stretch this word. R-r-r-a-b-b-i-t. Now, everyone, please stretch with me. R-r-r-a-b-b-i-t. Again, r-r-r-a-b-b-i-t.*

*I've drawn a magic line here for us to write the sounds that we hear in the word* rabbit, *but first Spencer will demonstrate how to stretch this word two different times, then he will lead you in stretching this word with him. Spencer, in your loudest voice please show us how to stretch* rabbit.

Encourage your Stretching Star to go slowly and speak loudly. Make sure he/she stretches the word correctly twice before letting the students join in.

**Teacher:** *Thank you, Spencer. Could all of you please join Spencer now as he stretches the word* rabbit?

Provide a few moments for your Stretching Star and the class to stretch the word, watching that your leader is indeed using his or her voice to lead the students.

If your Stretching Star stumbles or needs assistance, repeat the process from the beginning until the student is successful.

**Teacher:** *Now let's write the sounds that we hear. Spencer, could you please repeat the beginning sound in our word? Thank you.*

*Who knows what letter makes that r-r-r sound? Yes, it is the letter* r. *Could you please come up here and write a lowercase* r *at the beginning of our magic line? Thank you.*

Continue by having your Stretching Star stretch the word again, and ask the students what other sounds they hear. When they have written all of the sounds that they can recognize, add the rest of the sounds to spell the word correctly.

## Stretching Table Star

Some teachers have found it helpful to ask one student at each table to be the Stretching Table Star for one week. Again, it places responsibility on one student to be engaged, speak loudly, and show that he or she knows the process.

These Stretching Table Stars help the students at a particular table stretch one word a day. They stand to stretch the word, and the rest of the students at that table join in. This encourages independence from the teacher, and students take pride in what they can accomplish on their own. This is generally only necessary for August through the end of September.

# Write What You Hear

Students need to think independently and learn to take risks when stretching words and hearing sounds. The purpose of this mini-lesson is to provide a safe, non-threatening environment for students to practice writing the sounds they hear in words.

**Type of Mini-Lesson:** Interactive

**Length:** 8–12 minutes

**Materials:** a small chalkboard and chalk or whiteboard and marker for each student

## Process

**Teacher:** *Today I am going to stretch some words and I would like you to write the sounds you hear. The first word is* baby. *Buh-buh-buh-a-b-y. Write on your boards the letter that makes the buh sound. When you have your letter written, hold your boards up so I can see your letter.*

Provide time for students to say the sound, hear the sound, and write the letter.

**Teacher:** *Yes, it is the letter* b. *A b is the first sound in the word* baby. *Show one another your boards. Now erase your b's.*

> *I'll stretch the word again. See if you can hear the next sound in the word* baby. *Buh-buh-buh-a-b-y. Write the letter that you think makes the sound.*

> *Show me your boards, please.*

> *Yes, it is the letter* a *that makes the ā sound.*

> *Show your boards to one another.*

> *Now erase your a's.*

> *I'll stretch the word again. See if you can hear the next sound after the* a *in* baby. *Buh-buh-buh-a-b-y. What letter makes that buh sound again? Please write that letter on your boards.*

**Teacher:**   *Show me your boards when you are ready.*

*Yes, it is the letter* b.

*This word has two* b*'s in it.*

*Show one another your boards.*

*Now you can erase your boards.*

*Okay, now we have one more sound in the word* baby.

*It's a bit tricky, so think before you write a letter.*

*Let me stretch that word one more time: Buh-buh-buh-a-b-y.*

*What letter makes that ē sound at the end of the word?*

*Write the letter on your boards.*

*Show me your boards.*

*I see some of you wrote the letter* e. *It certainly makes that sound, doesn't it? I see some of you wrote the letter* y. *The letter* y *is at the end of the word* baby. *Let's have everyone write the letter* y *on their boards. Show one another your letters. You can erase your boards.*

*Now let's stretch and write all of the letters that we hear in the word* baby. *Stretch with me. Buh-buh-buh-a-b-y. Write the letter that makes that first buh sound. Next to it write the letter that makes the ā sound. Now write the letter that makes the buh sound. Finally, write the letter that makes the ē sound. When you are ready, show me your boards with the word* baby.

*Great work today. When you are writing in your journals, please take the time to stretch the word, hear the sounds, and write the letters that make those sounds.*

   First Lessons for Beginning Writers © 2010 by Lola M. Schaefer, Scholastic Teaching Resources

# Specific Word Choice

Writers are wordsmiths. They create both artful and functional text by the correct placement of just the right word. The more specific the word choice, the stronger the images that the reader will read and see in his/her mind. The purpose of this mini-lesson is to show students the difference between general and precise word choice.

**Type of Mini-Lesson:** Interactive

**Length:** 5–8 minutes

**Materials:** overhead projector and marker or interactive whiteboard and pen

## Process

**Teacher:** *As writers, we want to always be as specific as we can be with our word choice. By specific, I mean that we want to select the best word to match what we see in our mind. For instance, a student could write this sentence: "The toddler held a bug in her hand."*

*That bug could be a ladybug, a butterfly, or a wasp. The reader doesn't really know and has to guess whether the toddler is in danger or not. However, if a student wrote, "The toddler held a live wasp in her hand," we would immediately be fearful that he or she might get stung.*

*Let's practice thinking of more specific words so, as we write, we will be aware of the words that we choose.*

*Please look up here. On the left side, I'm writing "General/Vague." I will list words underneath this heading that do not paint good pictures in the mind of a reader—words like* bug. *On the right side, I'm writing "Specific/Precise." We will list words here that do paint strong pictures in the mind of a reader—words like* ladybug, tarantula, bumblebee, praying mantis, *or* wasp.

Your transparency or interactive whiteboard should have a vertical line separating the two sets of words, and a horizontal line beneath them (see page 36).

Write one general term, such as *food* on the left side. Provide a sentence using that word: *The boy frowned when he saw the food.* Ask the students, "What are the names of some specific foods? Name some foods that you dislike." Write their responses so all can see. I usually stop after the students have named four or five specific examples. Continue the process with another two general words. Some of your general/vague choices can be: bug, car, clothes, worker, place, toy, game, room, or the choices listed below.

**Teacher:** *Today as you are writing, use words that are specific—that will paint an exact picture in your reader's mind.*

| General/Vague | Specific/Precise |
|---|---|
| food | cheese pizza, pears, lettuce, tomato soup, baked potato |
| animal | whale, holler monkey, iguana, bulldog, chipmunk, grizzly bear |
| house | cabin, houseboat, mansion, mobile home, shack |

## Accountability Pays Off

Whenever you offer this mini-lesson before students write, make sure that at the end of writing workshop you say, "Since today we were all thinking about using specific words, go back and reread your writing. Circle the two most specific words that you included." Some students will be circling, and other students will be erasing and changing general/vague words to more specific ones. Ask a few students to share one of their specific words.

# Listening for Action Words

When students discover strong active verbs in literature, they are much more likely to use them in their own writing. The purpose of this mini-lesson is to help students recognize specific action words and comment on how they add strong images and interest to the text.

**Type of Mini-Lesson:** Literature-based

**Length:** 5–8 minutes

**Materials:** a page from a published book that holds interest for your students and is jam-packed with strong active verbs. I will be using page 17 from *This is Your Life Cycle* by Heather Lynn Miller (Clarion, 2008).

## Process

Select a page from a book that the children have heard several times and know well.

**Teacher:** *Today I would like you to listen with your writer's ear for action words: words that tell us how someone or something moved or what they did. For instance, when I say, "The mosquito buzzed in my ear," the action word is* buzzed. *It tells what the mosquito did.*

*Active verbs are at the center of all good writing. I'm going to read one page of this book, a book we all know well. Listen and enjoy.* (Read the page and then stop.)

*Now I'm going to reread it again and stop after each sentence. Tell me the action words that you hear.*

After the first sentence, the students mention the word *wiggled*.

**Teacher:** *Yes, that's an action word. It says what Dahlia did.*

After the second sentence, the students mention the word *wiggled* again.

**Teacher:** *Yes, now the box turtle is telling us exactly where and how she wiggled.*

After the third sentence, the students mention the words *gobble* and *disappeared*.

**Teacher:** *Who was going to gobble Dahlia? Yes, the box turtle.*

*Who disappeared? Yes, Dahlia disappeared under a pile of dead leaves.*

*Our strong action words—or verbs—today were* wiggled, gobble, *and* disappeared.

*Today, as you write, use as many strong, specific action words as you can. They will make your writing pop on the page.*

## POP UP!

After independent writing time, ask students to go back and reread what they've written. Ask them also to find one strong action word—a word that made their writing pop. When they have one, they can pop up from their seat and share it with the class. You can also create a bulletin board titled "Pop-Up Action Words" and have students copy their strong verbs on small pieces of paper and add them to the board. In this way, we celebrate what students have accomplished and encourage their continued use of strong, specific verbs.

# POWerful Verbs

Strong, specific action words pack a punch. They add life and energy to writing. The purpose of this mini-lesson is to help students brainstorm more specific action words so they build a repertoire of verbs that can vitalize their writing.

> **Type of Mini-Lesson:** Interactive
>
> **Length:**     4–8 minutes
>
> **Materials:**     overhead projector and marker or interactive whiteboard and pen

## Process

**Teacher:** *We've been finding strong active verbs in published books. You all have made comments that these words help paint pictures or show you how something happened. Today, before we write, I'd like us to brainstorm some specific action words. For instance, one of us could write, "The custodian brought the plumbing supplies into the school." Can you tell how the custodian did that? Can you act out how he moved?*

Most students will tell you that they don't know if he carried the supplies, pulled them, or what, so it would be difficult to act it out.

**Teacher:** *Imagine that one of us wrote, "The custodian dragged the plumbing supplies into the school."*
*Now can you tell me how the custodian brought them in? Can you act out how he moved?*

Students will be anxious to show you how the custodian dragged the plumbing supplies.

**Teacher:** *Today let's pick one general action word—one that doesn't paint strong pictures. Let's use the word* went*: "The second-grade boy went into the lake." I really don't know how he entered the lake. What could we say instead of* went*?*

As students brainstorm more specific verbs, write them down where they all can see them. For instance, some of their answers may be *ran, jumped, cannonballed, dove, dropped,* or *plopped.*

Other words that work well for this mini-lesson in grades K and 1 are: *walked, told, looked, ate,* or *felt.*

**Teacher:** *Today, as you write, try to use specific action words. They will add interest and paint pictures in your readers' minds.*

## Share Your Best

After your students have completed their writing for the day, ask them to go back and reread what they've written. Say: "Please circle your strongest action word—the one that will paint a picture for your reader."

Some students will be circling, and some will be erasing and inserting a stronger verb for a weaker one. Provide time for both activities. Then ask students to volunteer some of their stronger action words. If you repeat this activity at the end of writing time for a week or more, your students will be committed to using more specific verbs in their writing.

# Detail Hunt

To prepare students to include details in their prewriting, whether that is a picture or a simple written organizer, it is helpful to first have them find details. The purpose of this mini-lesson is to help students focus on details on the cover of a book. It fosters students' awareness of what detail is and how it adds meaning.

**Type of Mini-Lesson:** Literature-based/Interactive

**Length:**      5–8 minutes

**Materials:**   a cover of a picture book that has at least 6–10 details, but not one that is so busy that it's overwhelming to students; chart paper and marker or whiteboard and pen

## Process

The teacher holds up the cover of a picture book. For this lesson I will be using *Chicken Said, "Cluck!"* by Judyann Ackerman Grant (HarperCollins, 2008).

**Teacher:**   *Today we're going to hunt for details. Details are pieces of information that add meaning, interest, or zip to a picture or a piece of writing. Details can tell us where something happens or how something happens. Details can help us decide if someone is surprised, confused, angry, or excited. Details can show us if someone is sitting, standing, or leaning.*

   *Look at this book cover. We see a chicken and some sort of insect looking at one another.*

   *The **who** is a chicken and an insect. The **what** is looking at one another. Now study the picture. Look for details that tell us where they are, or what else they're doing, or what time of day it is. Take a moment to look and think.*

Provide at least 1–2 minutes when no one talks and everyone is studying the book cover.

**Teacher:**   *Who would like to mention one detail?*

As children mention details, place a tally mark on chart paper or on a whiteboard to be counted at the end.

Student responses might be:

>It is daytime.
>
>Grass and plants are near them.
>
>Blue/purple flowers are blooming.
>
>The antennae on the bug are standing up.
>
>The chicken is leaning forward.
>
>The word *cluck* is written in orange letters.
>
>The rest of the title is written in green letters.
>
>The insect has more legs than the chicken.
>
>The bug looks a little frightened.
>
>The fence looks old, like it's been there for a while.
>
>There are either seeds or little stones on the ground.
>
>The chicken's beak is yellow-orange.

If students struggle at the beginning of this mini-lesson, ask a few questions to guide them to discovering the details.

**Teacher:** *You did a wonderful job of finding details today. Let's count these marks and learn how many you discovered. Now, how many details do you think we need to include today in our own prewriting pictures? (Try to guide them to a realistic number such as 2, 3, or 4.) Let's remember what a detail is. A detail tells us more about the place, the time, what someone is doing, how someone feels, what something looks like, or what is happening. Let's see if you can include two to four details in your prewriting pictures today.*

 First Lessons for Beginning Writers © 2010 by Lola M. Schaefer, Scholastic Teaching Resources

# Listening for Detail With a Writer's Ear

Student writers are brimming with details. The purpose of this mini-lesson is to help them recognize the different kinds of details so they will add interest and zip to their writing.

> **Type of Mini-Lesson:** Literature-based
>
> **Length:** 5–8 minutes
>
> **Materials:** a picture book that has many specific details—details that not only describe the appearance of something but how something happens; chart paper and marker or white page displayed on interactive whiteboard and pen

## Process

For this mini-lesson example, I'm using *Fletcher and the Falling Leaves* by Julia Rawlinson (Greenwillow, 2006). I would select just one page from this book to read out loud. (Strong choices are pages 4, 7, 10, 11, 14, or 17, counting only pages with text.)

**Teacher:** *Today I would like you to listen with your writer's ear for details. A detail is not one word but a group of words that adds interest or zip to the writing. For instance, "Little lost leaves spun everywhere" is a detail. It adds interest and paints a picture that a few smaller leaves were spinning all by themselves.*

*The details you hear today will paint pictures in your minds. So shut your eyes and listen carefully. I will read one page from the book* Fletcher and the Falling Leaves *two times. The first time, I'll read the page all the way through. The second time, I will pause and give you an opportunity to tell me the details that you hear.*

Read the selected page out loud all the way through. Now read it again and stop after every two sentences so students can tell you which details they hear. You can prompt them with questions like the following:

> *Which words painted a picture in your mind?*
> *Which words told you how something moved or what it did?*
> *Which words told you what Fletcher did?*
> *Which words added interest for you?*

As students list details, print them on the chart paper or the interactive whiteboard. Once you have three or more details, reread the list to the students.

**Teacher:** *You listened well today. Look how many details you found. The author wrote these details to add meaning to the writing. Today, as you write, look for opportunities to add interesting details.*

# Drawing With Detail

When students draw a picture before they write in their journals, they are organizing their thoughts. This is an important THINK time for them. The purpose of this mini-lesson is to show students how to add details to their pictures so that later they will include some of those same details in their writing.

**Type of Mini-Lesson:** Demonstration

**Length:**     5–9 minutes

**Materials:**    large journal page or chart paper, pencil, and crayons

## Process

**Teacher:** *I want to write today about the rainbow that I saw outside my house last night. First I need to draw a picture to organize my thoughts. I want to include my **who** in the picture. Since I was outside, I am going to draw myself standing on the grass.*

Draw your picture as you think aloud.

> *Next, I need the **what** in my picture. I'm going to draw the rainbow in front me in the sky. Now I have both the **who** and the **what** in my picture. I want to include both of those in my writing.*
>
> *I would also like to add some details. My dog Duke was standing next to me, so I'm going to draw him next to me.*
>
> *We were standing under the big tree in our front yard. I will add that tree to the picture.*
>
> *The sun was shining behind the rainbow. I will add the bright sun, too. Since I was amazed by the rainbow, I need to draw my mouth and eyes opened wide.*

Use many different colors for the details in your picture. When you're finished, ask students to mention their favorite details. Then end by having them count how many details you added to your picture.

**Teacher:** *Today as you draw your pictures for your journal writing, make sure you have your **who** and **what** and then try to add at least two details to your drawing. I know that some of you will add more, but let's see if we all can add two interesting details to our pictures.*

 *First Lessons for Beginning Writers* © 2010 by Lola M. Schaefer, Scholastic Teaching Resources

# Find My Details

For students to include details in their writing, they first need to put those details in their organizational drawing. By discovering details in the pictures of their classmates, students see the importance and purpose of adding detail. This mini-lesson makes students aware of how details add interest to both pictures and, later, to their writing.

**Type of Mini-Lesson:** Student Demonstration

**Length:** 5–8 minutes

**Materials:** a picture from a student's journal

## Process

As you're observing students working on their journal pictures, look for one picture that has the **who**, the **what**, and some detail. Ask that student if he or she would be willing to show the picture to the class and have other students find details in it. After the student is seated or standing in front of the rest of the class, begin this process.

**Teacher:** *Hannah, could you please tell us who you are writing about today?*

After the student responds, ask: "And, what is he or she doing?" Provide time for the student to answer and point to the parts of the picture that show the **what**.

**Teacher:** *Students, study this writer's picture carefully. We can see the **who** and the **what**, but what other details do you see in Hannah's picture?*

If students do not offer details immediately, prompt them with questions like these:

> *Can you tell if it is day or night? How?*
> *What are some of the smaller objects in this picture?*
> *Can you see any clothing on the people? What kind?*
> *Is anyone carrying something? What is it?*

For every detail that students mention, hold up a finger. When the last detail is mentioned, tell the writer how many details he or she has included in the picture.

**Teacher:** *Hannah, which of these details do you think you will add to your writing today?*

Depending on the experience and age of the writer, encourage him or her to add one or two details in words.

**Teacher:**    *Students, which detail added the most meaning for you in this picture?*

Allow time for several students to offer details.

**Teacher:**    *When you return to your pictures today, go back and decide how you can add one or two details to your picture and then to your writing.*

# Adding Zip

Emergent writers enjoy adding detail to their writing. The purpose of this mini-lesson is to provide practice in revising a basic sentence to include an informational detail about the **how** or **why**.

**Type of Mini-Lesson:** Interactive

**Length:**       8–12 minutes

**Materials:**    chart paper and marker, overhead projector and marker, or interactive whiteboard and pen

## Process

Write the following sentence and these words below it where everyone can see them. Read aloud the sentence.

*The fish swam away.*

*How?*                          *Why?*

**Teacher:**    *How could a fish swim away?*
*It could leap over a rock and swim away.*
*A fish could swish its tail and glide away.*
*Can you tell me ways that a fish could swim away?*

Write down at least three responses from students so everyone can see them.

**Teacher:**    *Why did the fish swim away?*
*The fish swam away to avoid the jaws of the alligator.*
*The fish swam upstream to make a nest.*
*Can you tell me some other reasons that a fish might swim away?*

Write down at least three responses from students so everyone can see them.

**Teacher:**    *I'm going to revise my sentence and add either how the fish swam away or why the fish swam away. I've decided to add why he swam away.*

Write the following sentence so everyone can see it: "The bluegill swam away when he saw the snapping turtle in the creek."

**Teacher:** *Why did the fish swim away?*

**Students:** *Because he saw a snapping turtle.*
*Because he didn't want the snapping turtle to get him.*

**Teacher:** *I'd like each of you to revise this sentence: The fish swam away. Add either **how** the fish swam away or **why** he swam away.*

Provide 3–4 minutes for students to revise the sentence. When they complete their work, have each student turn to a partner and read his or her sentence. Ask partners to tell the writers what additional information was added. After the sharing, ask for a show of hands.

**Teacher:** *How many of you added a detail about **how** the fish swam away?*
*How many of you added a detail about **why** the fish swam away?*
*Did anyone add both **how** and **why**?*
*Today in your writing look for opportunities to add **how** something happened or **why** it happened.*

# Details Add a Lot

Students need to know what details add to a piece of writing. They can add factual information, explain the how or why, paint pictures, or describe. When students can identify the intent of details, they more readily add them to their own writing. The purpose of this mini-lesson is to have students identify details and state what kind of information each adds to the text.

**Type of Mini-Lesson:** Interactive

**Length:** 6–12 minutes

**Materials:** chart paper and marker, overhead and marker, or interactive whiteboard and pen, large index cards

## Process

Be prepared to write each of the sentences below so everyone can see it.

> *On February 10, Jill met her grandmother at the Washington Monument.*
> *The octopus squirted ink, and the water looked like the night sky.*
> *She made her room brighter by hanging posters on the walls.*
> *The sunflower stood taller than his bike.*
> *She held her breath and jumped.*
> *The German shepherd wagged his tail when he heard his master's voice.*
> *The cook added two teaspoons of cinnamon to the cookie dough.*
> *She ran inside when the rain poured from the sky.*

Write each of the following phrases on a separate index card: *Adds Facts; Tells How; Tells Why; Paints a Picture; Describes.* Then place the cards in plain view of students.

**Teacher:** *We've been finding details in pictures and in sentences. Writers add details for the reader. Look at these five cards.*

Point to the cards one at a time and explain each phrase.

**Teacher:** *Sometimes a writer adds a detail to tell the reader a fact. It might be an exact time or place or amount. It's real information about a real event or person.*
 *Other times an author adds a detail to tell how something happened. The detail might say how a boy bounced a ball or how a bear ran through the woods.*

*A detail can explain why something happened. It could tell the reader why a boy ran into a house or why a girl wouldn't speak to her friend.*

*Some details paint picture with words. They make us see things in our heads or feel things in our hearts.*

*Details can also describe. They might tell the size, shape, or color of an object. They might tell us how long something is, or how quiet it is.*

Write one of the sentences listed on page 49 so all students can see it. Read it to the class two times. (I will use the first sentence as the example: *On February 10, Jill met her grandmother at the Washington Monument.*)

**Teacher:**  *Who is this sentence about? Yes, Jill. What did Jill do? Yes, she met her grandmother. I see some additional information in the sentence. Let me read it again. There are two details in this sentence. Can someone read one of the details? Yes, "On February 10" is a detail. Can someone tell us why the author added that information? What does it do? Does it tell us a fact? Does it tell us how they met? Does it tell us why they met? Does it paint a picture of what it looked like that day? Or does it describe Jill or her grandmother?*

### One a Day

To keep the mini-lesson focused and brief, only work with one sentence a day. Provide a thorough and supportive experience. For better comprehension, continue with another sentence for each consecutive day. If, after completing all sentences, you feel that your students need more practice, create a few more sentences and continue the process for another five days.

Provide time for discussion. When a student mentions that February 10 is an exact day, explain how that makes it factual information: The writer added a specific time—when this happened—with that detail.

**Teacher:**  *Does anyone see another detail in this sentence? Yes, "at the Washington Monument" is another detail. Can someone tell us why the author added that information? What does it do? Does it tell us another fact? Does it tell us how they met? Does it tell us why they met? Does it paint a picture of what it looked like that day? Or does it describe Jill or her grandmother?*

Again, provide time for discussion. When a student mentions that the Washington Monument tells us exactly where they met—the place—explain how that makes it factual information.

**Teacher:**  *Today as you write, think about adding details. Decide what information you would like to share with your audience. Some of you might add a fact to your writing, and others might add the how or why. Some of you might paint a picture with words, and yet others might describe the size, shape or color of an object.*

# What Does Your Detail Add?

Students need practice in adding detail to an otherwise blah sentence. The purpose of this mini-lesson is to give them an opportunity to practice adding detail and understand the kind of information that detail provides to the reader.

**Type of Mini-Lesson:** Interactive

**Length:**  8–12 minutes

**Materials:**  one of the "blah" sentences below, chart paper and marker or interactive whiteboard and pen, paper and pencil

> *The dog barked.*
>
> *Juan hid.*
>
> *Elise saw a rainbow.*
>
> *The plane rose into the air.*
>
> *Rabbits hopped.*
>
> *Joel's neighbor waved.*
>
> *The stars shone.*

## Process

Display one of the "blah" sentences so all students can easily see it.

**Teacher:**  *I'm going to read this sentence to you two times.*
*Please listen: The dog barked.*

Repeat the sentence.

**Teacher:**  *I think this is a boring sentence. It has no detail.*
*I don't know how the dog barked.*
*I don't know why the dog barked.*
*I don't know where he was when he barked.*
*I don't know who or what he barked at.*
*I would really like a detail or two.*
*We know that details can add facts:*
*The dog barked non-stop from 10 a.m. until 6 p.m.*
*We know that details can tell the reader how something happened:*
*The dog stood at the screen door and barked again and again.*

*Details can tell the reader why something happened:*
*The dog barked when the mailman walked up the sidewalk.*
*Details can paint a picture in our minds:*
*The dog barked so much that our eyes crossed and our toes curled.*
*And, we know that details can describe:*
*The Cocker Spaniel puppy barked so much that he became hoarse.*
*I'm going to rewrite the sentence and add one detail.*

Write your sentence beneath the "blah" sentence so all students can see it.

*The dog stood on his hind legs and barked at the garbage truck*
*as it rumbled past.*

Read your sentence two times to students.

**Teacher:**  *Would someone come up here and underline one detail that I added to that sentence?*

If a student underlines *stood on his hind legs,* ask:

*What kind of information does that tell the reader?*
*Does it describe? Does it tell how? Does it tell why?*
*Does it give factual information? Or does it paint a picture?*

A student might tell you that it describes what the dog looked like when it barked. That would be correct. Another student might tell you that it tells how he barked. That could be correct, as well. And a student might say that detail paints a picture in our minds. That, too, could be correct.

If a student underlines "at the garbage truck as it rumbled past," ask: "What information does that detail give the reader?" Repeat the above choices, if necessary. A student may say that this detail tells us why he barked. That is correct.

**Teacher:**  *I would like all of you to now rewrite or revise this blah sentence and add one detail that will give the reader more information.*

Provide 2–4 minutes for students to write their own detailed sentence. Ask partners to read their sentences to each other. Request that the listener repeat the detail that the writer included and then tell what kind of information it added.

**Teacher:**  *Today as you write, look for opportunities to add details. It will add interest and zip to your work.*

# Detail Hunt in Our Work

Once students can readily find details and add them, it is time to hold them accountable for including details in their own writing. The purpose of this mini-lesson is to celebrate one child's achievement so all students will work harder to include more specific details in their writing, which will then improve its quality and interest.

**Type of Mini-Lesson:** Interactive

**Length:** 6–8 minutes

**Materials:** an entry from one student's journal that contains at least one or two details

## Process

Select a student to sit or stand in front of the class. Ask the other students to sit on the floor in front of this student. Have the featured student first tell the **who** and **what** in his or her writing; for example: *my dad and I fishing, my mom and I shopping, my dog and I playing tug-of-war,* or *my friend and I riding bikes.*

**Teacher:** *I'd like you to ask your friends to listen with a writer's ear as you read your journal entry two times. Then, ask them to tell you any details they heard in your writing. In other words, can they tell if this happened during the day or night? Where did this happen? Is anyone carrying anything? Do you see any expressions on the faces? Details add information to the **who** and **what**.*

The first time you have a student offer this mini-lesson, you might need to prompt with a few questions specific to the writing. After students have listed all the details that they hear, discuss their responses.

**Teacher:** *Which detail do you think is the most important? Which ones give specific information about what is happening?*

*Today, when you are writing in your journals, try to include at least one good detail. Remember, details add interest and zip to your writing. They help paint pictures for your reader.*

### Working With a Partner

After your students participate in Detail Hunt in Our Work several times, you can place them with partners to find the details in one another's writing. If a student's work does not have the designated one or two details, both students can discuss ways for the writer to add a detail or two during a revision.

# What Happened Next?

When students first write their thoughts, they may not be in the correct order. With a little practice, sequencing events becomes much easier. The purpose of this mini-lesson is to help students consider the importance of sequencing and how it adds meaning to their writing.

**Type of Mini-Lesson:** Literature-based

**Length:** 4–8 minutes

**Materials:** a nonfiction book or article that has a simple, yet recognizable sequencing of events. I am using *First the Egg* by Laura Vaccaro Seeger (Roaring Brook Press, 2007) for my example.

## Process

**Teacher:** *When we write, we need to tell things in the order they happen. For instance, what happens first? Do you pour milk and then get a glass out of the cupboard, or do you get the glass out of the cupboard first and then pour milk? Yes, first you need the glass and then you can pour.*

*What happens first? Do you take a bath and then run the water? Or do you run the water and then take a bath? Yes, of course, you need to run the water first and then take a bath.*

*This book—First the Egg—shows us the order in which things happen. Instead of two events, it shows us three events. I'll read the first series to you. Please, listen carefully.*

Read the first series of events that goes from egg to chick to chicken.

**Teacher:** *What happened first?*

**Students:** *The egg.*

**Teacher:** *Correct. What happened second?*

**Students:** *The egg hatched, and a chick appeared.*

**Teacher:** *Correct again. What happened next?*

**Students:** *The chick grew into a chicken.*

**Teacher:** *Yes, it did. I'd like to share one more series of events from this book. Listen carefully as I read.*

Read another series of events from the book. (I use the seed, seedling, flowering plant as an example.) Repeat the process from above. Students will share that the seed came first, then the sprout or seedling, and finally the flower.

**Teacher:** *As you write today, think about what happened first, second, and last. We call this sequencing—putting events in the order that they happened.*

# Sequencing the Facts

Student writers need to consciously think about ordering the information in their work. The purpose of this mini-lesson is to show them how to sequence information before they write.

> **Type of Mini-Lesson:** Demonstration
>
> **Length:**    5–9 minutes
>
> **Materials:**    interactive whiteboard and pen or chart paper and marker

## Process

**Teacher:**    *We have been studying the life cycle of a butterfly.* (Use any content subject that you and your class have been studying that will work for this sequencing mini-lesson.) *Before we write what we have learned, let's make a plan of the most important facts we want to include. Name one of the stages in the life cycle of a butterfly.*

Abbreviate and list the stages as students respond.

**Teacher:**    *Yes. At one point a chrysalis is formed. I'll write* chrysalis *in our plan. What's another stage of a butterfly's development? Yes, an egg. Let me add that to our plan. Can someone else name another part of this life cycle? A caterpillar is another stage. I'll add that to our list, as well. There's one more stage: the final stage of this development. Yes, the butterfly. I'll add that to our plan.*

> Chrysalis
>
> Egg
>
> Caterpillar
>
> Butterfly

**Teacher:** *Before we write, we need to decide if these stages are in the correct order. In other words, we want to start at the beginning of the life cycle and write about it until the end.*

*What happens first? Yes, a butterfly lays eggs. I'll put a 1 beside Egg. What happens next? Yes, a caterpillar hatches from the egg. I'll write 2 beside Caterpillar. What does the caterpillar do? Yes, it makes a chrysalis. I'll write 3 beside that word. And, finally, what emerges from the chrysalis? Yes, a butterfly. I'll put 4 beside that word.*

*Let's check our thinking. Is the egg the first stage? Is the caterpillar the second stage? Is the chrysalis the third stage? And, is the butterfly the final stage of development?*

Chrysalis 3

Egg 1

Caterpillar 2

Butterfly 4

**Teacher:** *Now we are ready to think about what we want to say about each of these stages. We know that our writing will be sequenced and make sense for our reader.*

*When you are writing, take time to think about which event happened first, second, third, and so on. If you sequence your writing, it will be easier for your audience to read and understand.*

# When Did That Happen?

The correct sequence adds meaning to both story and small-moment writing, as well as informational writing. The purpose of this mini-lesson is to provide practice to student writers so they can more easily sequence their own writing independently.

> **Type of Mini-Lesson:** Demonstration
>
> **Length:**      5–10 minutes
>
> **Materials:**    interactive whiteboard and pen or chart paper and marker

## Process

Write the five sentences below in the order shown. Make sure everyone can easily see them.

> *When Sammy touched Pepper's cage, the dog licked Sammy's hand.*
> *They looked at all of the dogs and cats.*
> *Sammy and his family visited the humane shelter.*
> *Sammy and his family adopted Pepper, and they all walked home together.*
> *One dog named Pepper sat up on his hind legs.*

**Teacher:** *We have been talking about sequencing a lot lately. Sequencing means to put events in the order in which they happened. Today I would like us to read, think, and sequence these sentences so they make sense. First let me read all of the sentences to you.*

Read the sentences two times to your students so they know what the writing is about.

**Teacher:** *What is this writing telling us? What is the focus?*
**Students:** *It's about Sammy getting a new dog.*
*It's about Sammy and his family going to the humane shelter.*
*It's about a dog named Pepper.*

**Teacher:** *Who is the main character? Who is doing something in this writing?*
**Students:** *Sammy.*
*Sammy and his family.*
*Pepper.*

**Teacher:** *Who adopts Pepper? Yes, Sammy and his family, so they are the main characters of this writing. What do they do first? Do they touch? Look? Visit? Or adopt first?*

**Student:** *First, they visited the humane shelter.*

**Teacher:** *Yes. That is what happened first. I'll write 1 in front of that sentence. After they visited, did they touch, look or adopt? What happened next?*

Continue with this process until students have correctly ordered all the sentences. In the end, the ordering will look like this:

*When Sammy touched Pepper's cage, the dog licked Sammy's hand.* 4

*They looked at all of the dogs and cats.* 2

*Sammy and his family visited the humane shelter.* 1

*Sammy and his family adopted Pepper, and they all walked home together.* 5

*One dog named Pepper sat up on his hind legs.* 3

**Teacher:** *As you write your small moments or stories today, think about what happened first, next, and after that. Try to sequence your events the way that it makes the most sense.*

## Another Day

Re-ordering these events is enough practice for one day. However, for reinforcement, you may choose to put these sentences with their sequenced numbers on display the next day and allow students to copy them in the correct order. As a celebration, provide time for each student to read the newly reorganized text to a partner.

*First Lessons for Beginning Writers © 2010 by Lola M. Schaefer, Scholastic Teaching Resources*

# Read to the Wall

Students need to reread their writing to confirm that it makes sense. Quite often, when they read it aloud to a friend or the class, they discover areas for improvement. The purpose of this mini-lesson is to show children the value of stopping and reading to the wall to improve meaning.

**Type of Mini-Lesson:** Demonstration

**Length:**      4–6 minutes

**Materials:**    current piece of teacher writing that contains a few errors, pencil

## Process

**Teacher:**    *Writers enjoy hearing their own words. It gives them a sense of accomplishment; they have completed something important. But there is another reason that writers like to listen to their writing. When we read out loud what we've written, we hear things with our writer's ear that we might not notice when reading silently. For instance, I always hear repetitions—words that I have used over and over again. I am then able to change some of those words so my writing is more fluent.*

*Sometimes when I read my writing out loud, I realize that there are no periods at the ends of my sentences. I then can go back and add periods so my writing makes more sense.*

*Other times when I read out loud, I hear silly things, like I have forgotten a word or two. After adding those words, my writing communicates what I want it to say.*

*And when I read out loud, I often notice if I use boring words. If so, I can revise and turn those boring words into words that paint pictures or add pizzazz to my writing.*

*Today I want to show you how to "read to the wall." I'm going to take my writing from today and stand close to the wall.*

Stand about 8–12 inches from a wall, a whiteboard, a door, or a cabinet. (Some children even like to read to the floor.)

**Teacher:**    *Now I'm going to read my writing out loud two times. But I'm not going to read loudly. I'm just going to read loud enough so I can hear my words when they bounce off the wall and come back to my ears.*

Demonstrate by reading a short passage two times.

**Teacher:**    *Oh, my writer's ear heard a place where I left out two words. Excuse me while I add those right now.*

Allow the class to watch you as you insert two missing words.

**Teacher:**    *And I kept using the word it, it, it. I need to change two of those words so my reader knows what I am saying.*

                     *Let me read the revised writing. Yes, it makes more sense than before.*

Read your piece out loud to the students. Show them what you revised at the wall.

**Teacher:**    *Starting today, you may read to the wall to see if your writing makes sense. Always remember to take your pencil with you to the wall so you can make revisions or edits that need to be made as you hear them.*

---

### Model, Model, Model

Students tend to mimic writing behaviors that we model. One mini-lesson on reading to the wall will introduce the strategy. However, it would be wise to repeat this procedure frequently in a two-week period so your students will begin to do it regularly.

---

# Celebration of Read to the Wall

Once students begin reading to the wall to check for meaning, it is wise to reinforce their efforts through celebration. The purpose of this mini-lesson is to show students that revision does improve meaning and that it is appreciated by an audience.

**Type of Mini-Lesson:** Student Demonstration/Interactive

**Length:** 8–10 minutes

**Materials:** writing from a student volunteer

## Revision Fever

Only allow one or two students a day to read their before-and-after revised writing. That alone will start a *revision fever* in your classroom. When students receive this positive feedback, they work harder at the wall to improve the quality of their writing.

## Process

Conduct this lesson after a few children have been reading to the wall.

**Teacher:**     *Did anyone make a change, a revision, at the wall today?*

When a student raises his or her hand, repeat the question.

**Teacher:**     *Did you make a change to your writing at the wall?*

If the student confirms this, then say:

**Teacher:**     *Could you please read the writing before the change?*

Provide time for the student to read.

**Teacher:**     *Now please read the revised, or changed, version.*

Provide time for the student to read. Then address the entire class.

**Teacher:**     *What did you hear in the revised reading that added meaning to the writing?*

Provide time for students to respond directly to the writer. After a student responds, ask for feedback.

**Teacher:**     *Did that revision improve the writing? How?*

In this way, the student receives positive feedback from peers on the revision that he or she made. The student now enjoys revision. The student, and the class, recognize that revision improves meaning and that an audience appreciates the changes.

# Revise Word Choice

Revision is a necessary part of the writing process. Student writers need to practice revision in brief mini-lessons so they build an understanding of how and when to use this effective tool. The purpose of this mini-lesson is to help student writers learn the process of changing weak vocabulary to improve the meaning of their writing.

**Type of Mini-Lesson:** Interactive

**Length:**     6–9 minutes

**Materials:**     interactive whiteboard and pen or chart paper and marker

## Process

Write this sentence so all students can easily see it: "The kid went into the store." Then read the sentence to the students two times.

**Teacher:**     *This sentence uses weak words. They do not paint clear pictures in my mind. Let me circle the words that are blah.*

Circle the words *kid, went* and *store.*

**Teacher:**     *Let's brainstorm more specific words for* kid, *and I will write them down beneath it. For instance, I'm going to suggest the word* toddler. *What are some other words that would paint a better picture than* kid?

Write the words that students offer. These might include *kindergartner, daughter, grandchild, four-year-old, second grader, princess,* and so on. Repeat this process for *went* and *store.* Choices might be *ran, rushed, hurried, scrambled, pushed, skipped,* and so on for *went.* Alternatives for *store* might be *grocery, hardware store, pet store, sports store,* or specific names of stores that the students know.

**Teacher:**     *I'm going to revise that sentence using more specific words so my readers will have stronger pictures in their minds.*

Write your own sentence so students can easily see it and read it out loud. You might write: "The second-grade boy hurried into the sports store and grabbed an autographed bat."

**Teacher:** *Now I would like each of you to revise this sentence and use specific words to paint stronger pictures for your readers.*

Provide 3–4 minutes for students to revise the sentence. Then have students share their revisions with a partner. Have the reader ask the partner to mention the most specific word in the revision.

After the sharing, ask the students, "Who heard a great revision of this sentence?"

When one student raises his or her hand, ask that student's partner to read his or her revision to the class. Ask the reader what word his or her partner appreciated in the revision. Repeat that process two or three times. More students will want to share, and that's good. You want to leave them with a positive attitude toward revision and sharing.

End by saying: "Today, as you write, try to use the most specific words—those that will paint strong pictures in your reader's mind."

# You and I

Grammar is difficult to teach to the emergent writer. Rules all by themselves hold little importance for these students. The purpose of this mini-lesson is to provide a strategy that can help student writers identify which pronoun to use at the beginning of a sentence.

**Type of Mini-Lesson:** Interactive

**Length:** 4–8 minutes

**Materials:** a display of the sample phrases shown below, paper and pencils, chart paper and marker or interactive whiteboard and pen

## Process

**Teacher:** *When writers begin a sentence talking about themselves and other people, they want their words to make sense. For instance, if I wrote about my dog Duke and me, I would begin my sentence "Duke and I." If I wrote about my husband and me, I would begin with "Ted and I." If I wrote about one of you, I would begin with "You and I."*
*Let me write those beginnings for you to see.*

*Duke and I*

*Ted and I*

*You and I*

*Can someone tell us about a pattern they see?*

Some students might mention that the other person or animal always comes first. Another student might mention that the word *I* always comes second.

**Teacher:** *Yes, we always put the other person's name or the animal first, then we use the pronoun I for ourselves.*
*What would you write at the beginning of a sentence about your grandma and you?*
*Please write how that would look at the beginning of a sentence (My grandma and I).*

Provide time for students to write. As you tour the room and look over shoulders, ask a student to write his or her words on the chart paper or interactive whiteboard for all to see.

**Teacher:** *What would you write at the beginning of a sentence about your pet hamster Olive and you?*

Repeat the process from above.

**Teacher:** *To end this mini-lesson, I'd like you to write an entire sentence about one of your friends and you, and what you like to do together. Let me show you what I mean.*

Write a sentence on the board, such as "Tracy and I like to talk about books we have read."

**Teacher:** *Now I'd like you to write your own sentence about you and a friend. Make sure you use our examples here to help you decide how to begin.*

Provide time for students to share their sentences with a friend. The listener needs to confirm whether or not the writer began the sentence correctly.

**Teacher:** *As you write today, remember how to begin sentences that talk about you and someone else.*

# Circle to Spell

Sometimes the reason that young writers do not even attempt to check or confirm their spelling is that they think they need to check every single word. We want to make spelling a manageable part of the editing process. The purpose of this mini-lesson is to show students how to identify the three or four most important words that need accurate spelling. We want to practice one habit of writers: checking or confirming spelling.

**Type of Mini-Lesson:** Demonstration/Interactive

**Length:**      9–15 minutes

**Materials:**   the passage below displayed on an interactive whiteboard with pen or on chart paper with marker

*Yestday, my frnd and I played at the park. The teeter-totter was brocn so we climed the monkey bars. I climed to the top and it was high like a mounten. We want to go back today.*

## Process

**Teacher:**   *Here is a piece of writing.*

Show writing from above so all students can see.

**Teacher:**   *Listen while I read it out loud.*

Read the piece two times so everyone can hear.

**Teacher:**   *This is a fine piece of writing. It has a **who** and **what**. It has specific words like* teeter-totter, yesterday, monkey bars, mountain and today. *Let's look at the words carefully now. Let's pretend that we wrote this. Before we give it to a reader, we want to check the spelling of three or four important words. These are words that the reader will need to read correctly to understand all of the meaning. I'll read that first sentence again: "Yestday, my frnd and I played at the park." What word or words do you think we need to check or confirm for spelling?*

Invite a student to come and circle a word that he or she feels is misspelled. Do not worry if the student only sees one word. We want him or her to assume responsibility.

Continue the same process for the other three sentences. If your students circled *Yestday, frnd, brocn* and *climed*, that's a good start.

Invite students to volunteer to check or confirm the spelling of one of the words. Provide time for them to find these words. (See page 69 for places where students might find the correct spelling of the words.)

When students have found the correct spellings, invite them to cross out the misspelled word and above it add the corrected word. Again, if your students only identify two of the misspelled words, applaud their efforts. You may choose to circle the other words for another mini-lesson and invite them to find the correct spelling.

# Spell-Check

We want students to understand that spelling is important; it helps carry the meaning of their written pieces. However, we don't want students interrupting their drafting to check the spelling of words. The purpose of this mini-lesson is to create a list of resources that students can use when checking or confirming the spelling of words during the editing process.

**Type of Mini-Lesson:** Interactive

**Length:** 8–12 minutes

**Materials:** chart paper and marker

## Process

**Teacher:** *We all know that spelling our words correctly in our writing helps the reader to understand what we've written. However, as you know, drafting is not the time to stop and correct or confirm the spelling of words. During drafting, we want to concentrate and get our ideas down on paper. But if you decide to publish a piece of writing—to let others read it—then you need to check or confirm the spelling of your important words.*

*I've noticed that some of you have been asking me or another student how to spell certain words. I would prefer that you check or confirm these words for yourself. That's one of the habits of writers; they assume responsibility for their own spelling.*

*Today I'd like us to look around the classroom and make a list of resources—books, posters, maps, and other items—that we can use when editing for spelling. Take a moment and study the walls. Look on the shelves and in your desks. What can we use to help us become stronger spellers?*

Provide a few moments for children to look and think.

**Teacher:** *When you see something that could help us, tell us your idea. I'm going to be making a list of these resources for the future.*

 First Lessons for Beginning Writers © 2010 by Lola M. Schaefer, Scholastic Teaching Resources

Students will start naming the following things:

the dictionary, the word wall, word lists, picture books, bulletin boards, personal dictionaries, spell-checks (on the computer using a word processing program or inexpensive hand-held spell-checkers available at office stores), and posters.

I try to lead them to unexplored possibilities until we have a list of at least 14–16 resources. Once students have created a list, add your name at the very bottom of the list.

**Teacher:**   *Since I want all of you to be responsible writers this year, you can only ask me to confirm the spelling of a word after you have used all of the other resources listed above my name.*

*If you have looked in all of these places and still can't find your word, I will be glad to help you. Let's post this list here on the wall. The next time you are going to check or confirm the spelling of a word, look at this list of ideas for where to look.*

# Periods at the End

Students write quickly when putting their thoughts on paper. They are concentrating on finding the words to say what is in their minds. They are stretching and hearing sounds and writing the letters that make those sounds. It's no wonder that they often forget to put periods at the ends of their sentences. The purpose of this mini-lesson is to provide students with a strategy to reread and add periods where needed.

---

**Type of Mini-Lesson:** Demonstration

**Length:**　　　8–10 minutes

**Materials:**　　writing sample shown below, interactive whiteboard and pen or chart paper and marker

*My aunt and uncle and three cousins came to our house*
*they drove here from Missouri we went canoeing and had a picnic at night*
*we played games like flashlight tag next we are going to drive to their house.*

---

## Process

Display the writing sample so all students can see it easily. Ask students to sit close to you.

**Teacher:**　*I would like to read this piece of writing to all of you. Please listen carefully.*

Read the writing sample two times.

**Teacher:**　*I like what the author has written. It sounds as if he or she had a good time with relatives. However, I can see that there is only one period at the end. Do you think there need to be more periods? Me, too.*

　　*Let me reread the entire first line: "My aunt and uncle and three cousins came to our house."*

　　*Who did what? Who means which people, and what means what they did.*

**Students:**　*My aunt and uncle and three cousins came to our house.*

**Teacher:** *Yes. That is a complete sentence; it tells who did what. I will place a period at the end of that sentence.*

*Let me read the words after that period. I'll read all of the next line: "they drove here from Missouri we went canoeing and had a picnic at night."*

*Let's look at that first word:* they. *What did they do?*

**Students:** *They drove here from Missouri.*

**Teacher:** *Yes. That's a complete sentence. It tells me who did what. I will place a period at the end of that sentence.*

Continue this process, always starting with the first word after the last period until all of the periods have been added.

End the mini-lesson by saying: *The next time you write, try this. Go back and reread all of your writing. Find your first complete sentence by looking for who did what. When you have a sentence that tells you who and what happened, place a period at the end. Start with the next word and find your next who and what happened. Place a period at the end of that sentence, too.*

## A Mini-Lesson on Capital Letters

After the students have added periods to this writing sample, save it for the next day. At that time, review how all sentences begin with a capital letter. Using this revised example, coach the students as they add capital letters at the beginning of each sentence.

# Capitals First

Student writers know that every sentence needs to start with a capital letter, but sometimes they forget this in the rush to get their ideas down on paper. The purpose of this mini-lesson is to have them return to their writing and edit for capital letters at the beginning of each sentence.

**Type of Mini-Lesson:** Interactive

**Length:**    5–8 minutes

**Materials:**    sample below written on chart paper with a marker or on an interactive whiteboard with a pen

*last night I played cards with my grandpa. we started with Crazy Eight. he beat me three times so we switched to Slap Jack. we played nine games of Slap Jack, and I won them all. what a good night!*

## Process

Display the above paragraph on chart paper or on the interactive whiteboard so all students can easily follow as you read it out loud. Read it twice so they are familiar with the passage.

**Teacher:**    *We have been talking about the use of capital letters at the beginning of some words. Can someone tell me one of the times we use a capital letter at the beginning of a word?*

**Students:**    *Names of people begin with a capital letter.*

        *Sentences begin with a capital letter.*

        *Names of streets and mountains start with a capital letter.*

        *My dog's name—Trixie—starts with a capital.*

**Teacher:**    *I'm glad that you remember so much about capital letters. Sometimes writers forget to start each sentence with a capital letter. But that's okay, because we can always go back and add them.*

        *In this piece of writing, the author forgot to capitalize the first words of the sentences. Let's go back and add the capital letters.*

Invite a student to come up to the chart paper or interactive whiteboard.

**Teacher:** *Please point to the first word in the first sentence. Is it capitalized?*

**Student:** *No, it needs a capital L.*

**Teacher:** *Go ahead and cross out the lowercase l and write a capital L above it. Thank you. Could another volunteer come up here and show us the first word of the second sentence? Is it capitalized?*

**Student:** *No. It needs a capital W.*

**Teacher:** *Please cross out the lowercase w and write the capital W above it. How did you know that was the first word of the second sentence?*

**Student:** *I saw the period at the end of the first sentence.*

**Teacher:** *That's a good strategy. The first word of the next sentence begins after a period. Let's use that strategy as we continue to edit this writing for capital letters.*

Continue with this same procedure until the entire piece is complete.

**Teacher:** *I hope that you take time today to reread your writing and check for capital letters at the beginning of each sentence. If you find that you've forgotten one or more, add them.*

## Adapt to Student Work

To repeat this kind of mini-lesson in the future, ask a student for permission to use his or her writing for this activity. Display the student's work and have him or her read it twice to the class. Ask the class to help the student go back, check, and add any needed capital letters. When we use student work in a positive way, as an example of what we all need to do, the students remember the strategy and use it more frequently.

# Peer Critique: Meaning

We want students to assume responsibility for their writing. The purpose of this mini-lesson is to show student writers how to meet with a peer (a writing buddy) and check that their writing makes sense. This mini-lesson will then lead them to purposeful revision.

**Type of Mini-Lesson:** Interactive

**Length:**      4–8 minutes

**Materials:**   writing sample below written on chart paper, a transparency, or on an interactive whiteboard

*Last night my friend and I went there. We saw the crocodiles crawl out. We watched the monkeys swing from one to another. We heard the macaws. We want to go back there soon.*

## Process

Display the writing sample where all students can easily see it and read it two times out loud.

**Teacher:**   *We're going to look at this writing now and decide what makes sense and what doesn't. Please listen as I read the first sentence again:*
                    *"Last night my friend and I went there."*
                    *Does that make sense? Do you know who went there? Do you know where they went?*

**Students:**  *We know that two people went somewhere.*
                    *We don't know where they went.*
                    *We don't know the name of the friend either.*

**Teacher:**   *So does all of the writing make sense?*

**Students:**  *No, some of the writing does not make sense.*

**Teacher:**   *As readers, we need to know where they went. Let's circle the words* went there. *We want to know where* there *is.*
                    *I'm going to read the next sentence. Please listen and tell me if it makes sense: "We saw the crocodiles crawl out."*
                    *Do you know what they saw? Do you know what the crocodiles were doing?*

**Students:**   *They saw crocodiles.*
            *They were crawling.*
            *We can't tell what they were crawling out of or into.*

**Teacher:**    *Does all of the writing make sense?*

**Students:**   *No. Most of the writing makes sense. We want to know where the crocodiles were crawling.*

**Teacher:**    *As readers, we are a bit confused. We need to ask the writer where the crocodiles crawled out from. Let's circle the words* crawl out.

            *Please listen as I read the next sentence: "We watched the monkeys swing from one to another."*

            *Do we know what they watched? Do we know what the monkeys did and where they did it?*

Students will note that the narrator and his or her friend watched monkeys. That part makes sense. They will also state that they know that the monkeys swung, but they're not sure where.

**Teacher:**    *Let's circle the words* from one to another. *We need to ask the writer where the monkeys were swinging. That part of the sentence is unclear and does not make sense.*

            *I'll read the next sentence. Please listen carefully to see if it makes sense: "We heard the macaws."*

            *Do we know what the narrator and friend heard?*

Students will tell you that they heard the macaws. They will say that this sentence does make sense. The students might also add that we don't know anything about the sound that the macaws were making. The writing does not need that sound to make sense, but it would be a great detail to add.

**Teacher:**    *Now I'll read the last sentence. Listen and decide if it makes sense: "We want to go back there soon."*

            *Do we know who wants to go back there? Do we know where they want to go?*

Students will share that they do know who: the narrator and the narrator's friend. That makes sense. They will also mention that they still don't know where they went and where they want to return. That part of the sentence is confusing and does not make sense.

**Teacher:**    *I agree that the last part of that sentence does not make sense. I will circle the words* back there. *We would need to ask the writer where they want to return.*

**Teacher:** *This is a practice piece. But if it were one of your pieces of writing, and your friend helped you circle places that did not make sense, then you, as the writer, would need to go back and rewrite the confusing places until all of the writing made sense.*

*Today, when you complete your writing, ask a friend to help you decide if your writing makes sense. If your friend marks a place where your writing is unclear, make sure you go back and rewrite that sentence until the meaning is clear to your friend.*

### Using Student Writing

You can use a short piece of student writing for a review of this mini-lesson in the future, but always ask the student's permission. Select a piece that makes sense most of the time and only has one or two places that need revision. Ask the student to read his or her writing to the class two times, then have the student go back and reread each sentence and ask the class if it makes sense or not. Place responsibility on the students, so they learn the procedure for helping one another with meaning.

# Peer Critique: Focus

We want students to assume responsibility for their writing. The purpose of this mini-lesson is to show student writers how to meet with a peer and check that their writing stays focused. This mini-lesson will then lead students to purposeful revision.

**Type of Mini-Lesson:** Interactive

**Length:** 5–10 minutes

**Materials:** writing sample below displayed on chart paper, a transparency, or on an interactive whiteboard

*Yesterday, my cat Whiskers ran away. I saw her leap through the kitchen window and jump into the flowerbed. Whiskers likes digging in the flowerbed. A car horn frightened her and she raced across our yard and into the woods. I don't like to go into the woods. I haven't seen my cat for the past three days. I miss Whiskers.*

## Process

Display the above writing so that all students can see it easily. Then read the writing sample out loud two times.

**Teacher:** *We're going to look at this writing now and decide what sentences stay on the focus. First of all, we need to state the focus of this writing. What is this writing about?*

**Students:** *It's about how Whiskers the cat ran away.*

**Teacher:** *That is correct. The focus is how Whiskers ran away. We want to keep any writing that describes how or when she ran away. We want to delete, or cross out, any writing that does not add information about the focus.*

*Please listen as I read the first sentence again: "My cat Whiskers ran away." Does that sentence give us information about our focus?*

**Students:** *Yes, it does.*

**Teacher:** *Good. Let's keep all of those words. Now listen as I read the next sentence. "I saw her leap through the kitchen window and jump into the flowerbed."*

*Does that sentence tell us something about when or how Whiskers ran away?*

**Students:**   *Yes, it says how she left the house.*

**Teacher:**   *I agree. It gives us information about how the cat left the house.*
*I will now read the next sentence. Listen carefully:*
   *"Whiskers likes digging in the flowerbed."*
   *Does that tell us when or how Whiskers ran away?*

**Students:**   *No, it doesn't say anything about the cat running away.*

**Teacher:**   *I agree. It is extra information that does not stay on the focus. Could*
*a volunteer come up here and draw a line through that sentence?*
*It does not belong in this writing.*

Continue the process, reading each sentence one at a time. Students will tell you that the sentence "I don't like to go into the woods" does not stay on the focus either. Ask a student to draw a line through that sentence, too.

After reading and considering each sentence, continue.

**Teacher:**   *If this were your writing and a friend helped you decide what parts*
*were on focus and what parts weren't, you could then draw a line*
*through those groups of words or sentences that were off focus. If you*
*were to publish this writing, you could rewrite it and omit, or leave*
*out, these two sentences.* [Point to the two sentences with lines drawn
through them.]

   *Today, when you complete your writing, you can ask a writing*
*friend to sit with you and check that all of your writing stays on*
*your focus. Before you and your friend begin, make sure that you*
*read your writing out loud two times. Then tell your listener what*
*your focus is. Read each sentence and ask your friend if it stays on*
*your focus. If not, draw a line through the words that do not.*

## Before and After

To reinforce students' efforts, provide time for one or two students to share which words or sentences their writing buddies helped them eliminate. They also like to read the before and the after to show how their writing has become more focused. Again, the more frequently we celebrate student success in peer critiques, the more responsibility they will assume in the future.

# Peer Critique: Word Choice

We want students to assume responsibility for their writing. The purpose of this mini-lesson is to show student writers how to meet with a peer and check that they are using specific words in their writing. This mini-lesson will lead students to purposeful revision.

> **Type of Mini-Lesson:** Interactive
>
> **Length:**        5–10 minutes
>
> **Materials:**     writing sample below displayed on chart paper, a transparency, or on an interactive whiteboard
>
> *My <u>grandpa</u> and I go fishing together. We <u>row</u> out into <u>Pine Lake</u> and <u>drop anchor</u>. Grandpa puts <u>stuff</u> on our hooks and we <u>cast</u> our lines into the water. We sit still and watch our <u>bobbers</u>. If a fish <u>gets</u> the <u>bait</u>, it's time to <u>reel in</u> the line.*

## Process

Display the above writing so that all students can see it easily. Then read the passage out loud two times.

**Teacher:**    *We're going to look at this writing now and look at the underlined words. As writers, we always want to use words that paint pictures in the minds of our readers. We want to use specific words. For instance, the word* gobbled *paints a better picture than the word* ate. *The word* quilt *paints a better picture than* cover.*

*As I read one of the underlined words, let's decide if it paints a clear picture in our minds. If it doesn't, let's think of a more specific word to use.*

Students will tell you that *grandpa, row, Pine Lake, drop anchor, cast, bobbers, bait,* and *reel in* provide a clear picture for the reader. Circle those words that they identify as specific.

**Students:**    Stuff *is not a specific word. We can't see* stuff *in our minds.*

**Teacher:**    *What could the writer use instead of* stuff? *What would this grandpa put on their fishing hooks?*

**Students:**　*Worms.*

*Earthworms.*

*Nightcrawlers.*

*Bait.*

*Crickets.*

**Teacher:**　*Any of those words would paint a better picture than* stuff. *Good choices.*

Students will also mention that the word *gets* is not specific.

**Teacher:**　*What are some other words the writer could use instead of* gets?

**Students:**　*Nibbles.*

*Tugs on.*

*Bites.*

*Pulls on.*

*Gobbles.*

**Teacher:**　*All of these words paint a stronger picture than* gets. *Decide which one you would use.*

*Today, when you complete your writing, you can ask a writing friend to sit with you and circle two or three specific words in your writing. The two of you need to also look for a word or two that could be changed to paint even stronger pictures for your reader.*

## Caution

We want young student writers to assume responsibility for improving the quality of their writing. However, we do not want to create checklists for peer critique. These students need to sit with a partner to check for only one element of excellent writing. Do not overwhelm students and extinguish their love of writing by asking them to sit with a writing partner and check for four or more different craft features. Student writers in kindergarten and first grade begin by checking for one craft element. Then, as their skills improve, they can eventually be checking for two or three different features.